I0164764

Backyard
Bugs
& Creepy
Crawlies

Roly-Polies

Ashley Lee

Explore other books at:
WWW.ENGAGEBOOKS.COM

VANCOUVER, B.C.

e WWW.ENGAGEBOOKS.COM

Roly-Polies: Level 1
Backyard Bugs & Creepy Crawlies
Lee, Ashley 1995 –
Text © 2025 Engage Books
Design © 2025 Engage Books

Edited by: A.R. Roumanis

Text set in Epilogue

FIRST EDITION / FIRST PRINTING

All rights reserved. No part of this book may be stored in a retrieval system, reproduced or transmitted in any form or by any other means without written permission from the publisher or a licence from the Canadian Copyright Licensing Agency. Critics and reviewers may quote brief passages in connection with a review or critical article in any media.

Every reasonable effort has been made to contact the copyright holders of all material reproduced in this book.

LIBRARY AND ARCHIVES CANADA CATALOGUING IN PUBLICATION

Title: Roly-Polies / Ashley Lee.
Names: Lee, Ashley, author.
Description: Series statement: Backyard bugs & creepy-crawlies
Engaging readers: level 1, beginner.

Identifiers: Canadiana (print) 20250448542 | Canadiana (ebook) 20250448569
ISBN 978-1-77878-708-9 (hardcover)
ISBN 978-1-77878-717-1 (softcover)

Subjects:
LCSH: Roly-Polies—Juvenile literature.

Classification: LCC QL737.P94 C38 2025 | DDC J599.885—DC23

This project has been made possible in part by the Government of Canada.

Canada

Contents

What Are Roly-Polies?

Roly-polies are also called pillbugs. But they are not bugs.

Roly-polies are crustaceans (cruh-stay-she-ins). They are more closely related to crabs and lobsters than bugs.

What Do Roly-Polies Look Like?

Roly-polies are an oval shape. They have soft stomachs.

They are covered in a hard shell. It is often gray or brown.

7

Roly-polies have 14 legs. They also have long feelers.

Roly-polies have **gills** like fish. They can only be seen if the roly-poly is on its back.

Key Word

Gills: a special body part that lets underwater animals breathe.

Where Do Roly-Polies Live?

Roly-polies used to only live in Europe. Now they live all over the world.

10

Roly-polies live in places that are wet. But they cannot live underwater.

What Do Roly-Polies Eat?

Roly-polies mostly eat dead plants. They like wood, leaves, and fruits.

Sometimes they will eat living plants. This is not as common.

Roly-Poly Behavior

Roly-polies hide during the day. The sun dries them out.

They often hide under rocks or logs. They are more active at night.

Roly-polies can roll into a ball. This helps them stay safe from other animals.

It also helps them keep **moisture** in their bodies. This helps them stay alive.

Key Word

Moisture: a small amount of wetness.

16

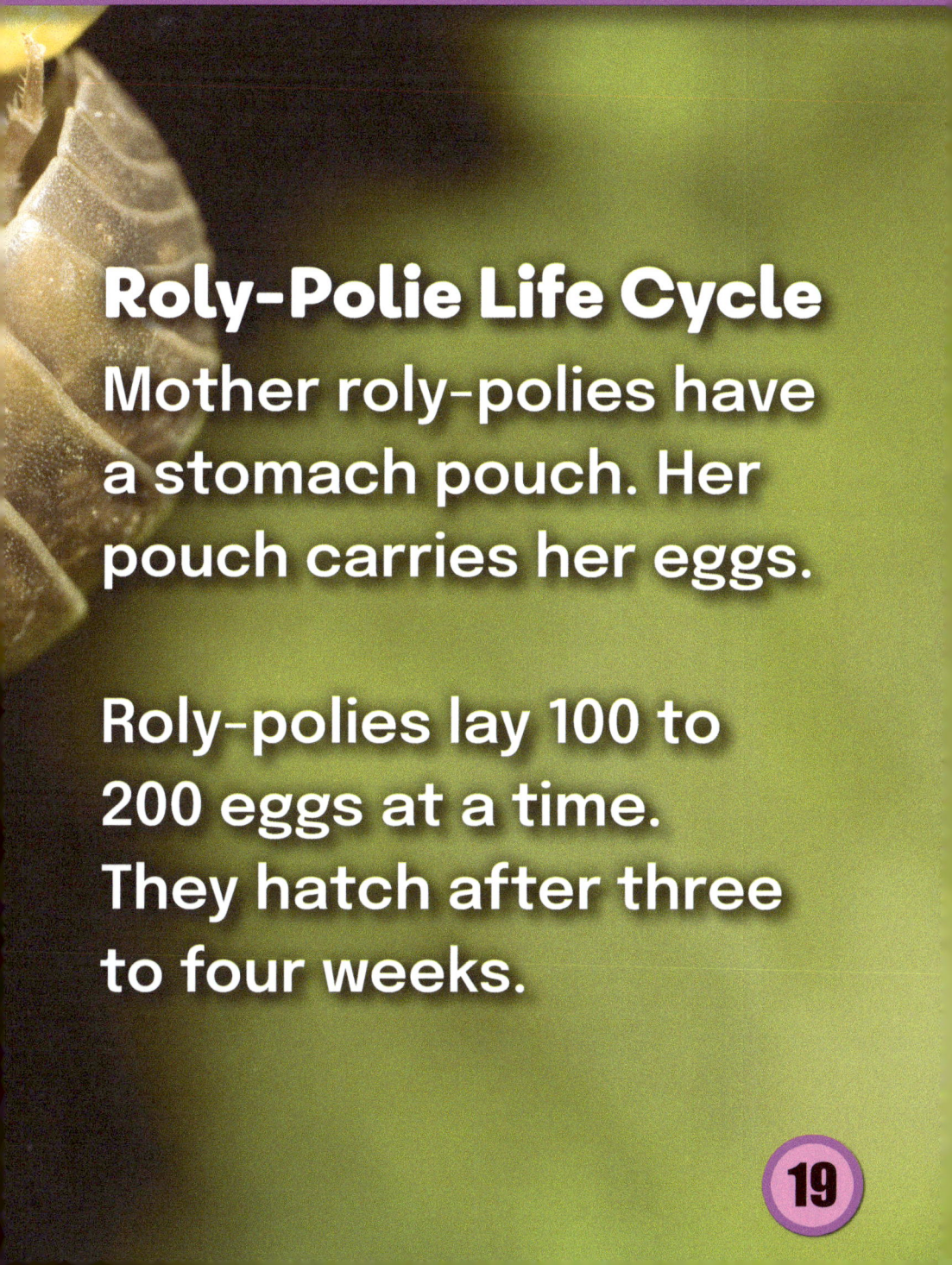

Roly-Polie Life Cycle

Mother roly-polies have a stomach pouch. Her pouch carries her eggs.

Roly-polies lay 100 to 200 eggs at a time. They hatch after three to four weeks.

Baby roly-polies often stay in their mother's pouch for another one or two weeks.

Most roly-polies live for about two years. Some live for five years.

Fun Facts

Roly-polies
do not pee.

Roly-polies can turn blue
when sick.

22

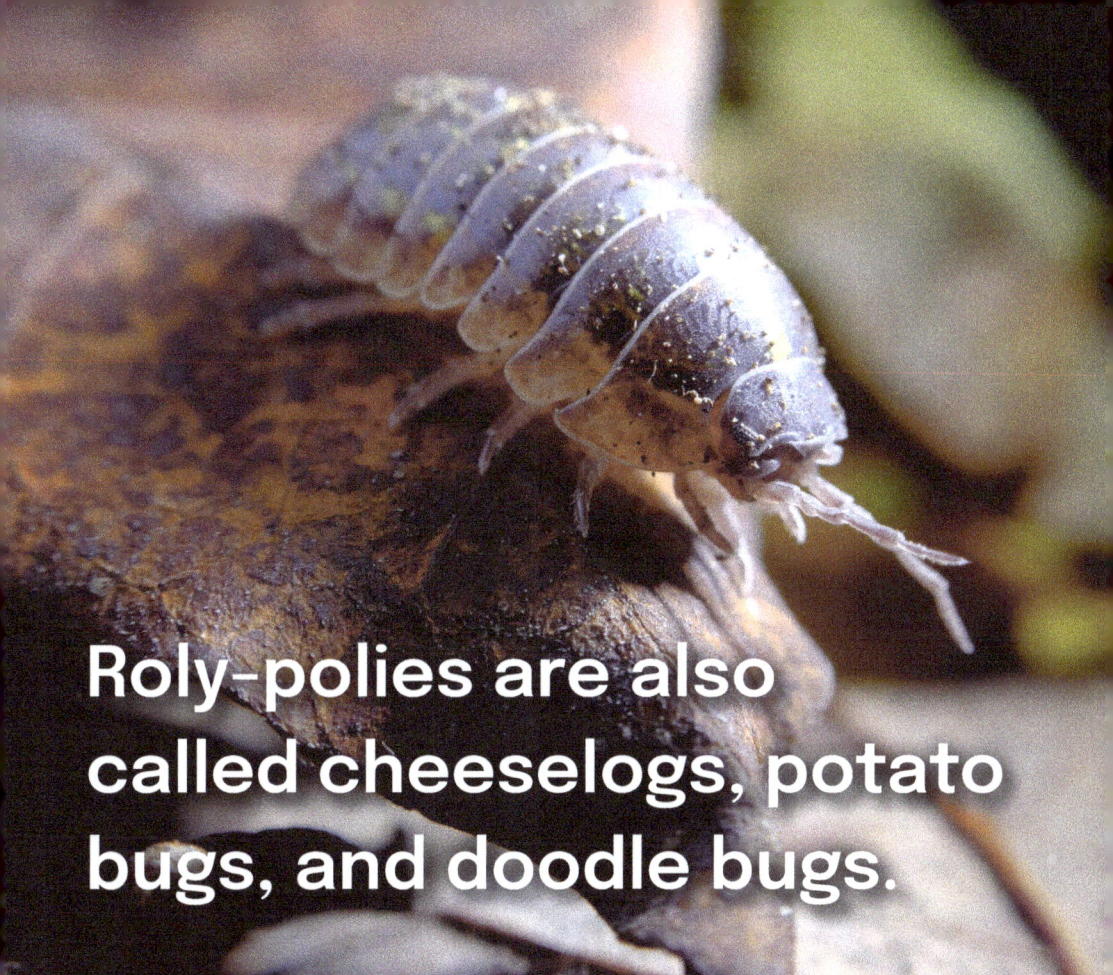

Roly-polies are also
called cheeselogs, potato
bugs, and doodle bugs.

Roly-polies can drink from
both ends of their bodies.

Roly-polies have a lookalike called the sowbug.

Roly-polies will not bite, sting, or pinch you.

Roly-poly babies are often colorless. Baby rolie-polies are born with only 12 legs.

Are Roly-Polies Helpful or Harmful?

Roly-polies are helpful to Earth! Their poop helps keep soil healthy.

Healthy soil grows healthy plants. Healthy plants make food for everyone.

Are Roly-Polies in Danger?

Sometimes animals start to die out. They can disappear forever.

But roly-polies are not in danger of dying out. There are lots of them all over the world.

29

Quiz

Test your knowledge of roly-polies by answering the following questions. The questions are based on what you have read in this book. The answers are listed on the bottom of the next page.

1 Are roly-polies bugs?

2 Do roly-polies have soft stomachs?

3 Can roly-polies live underwater?

4 Do roly-polies hide during the day?

5 Will roly-polies bite, sting, or pinch you?

6 Does roly-poly poop help keep soil healthy?

Explore other books in the
Backyard Bugs & Creepy Crawlies series!

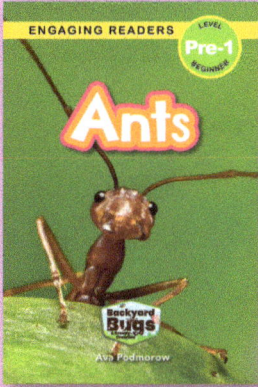

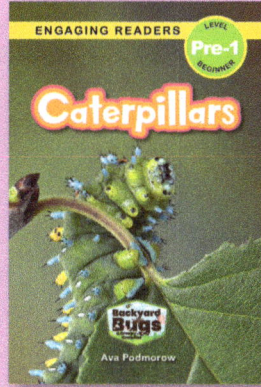

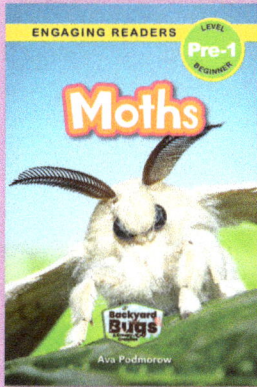

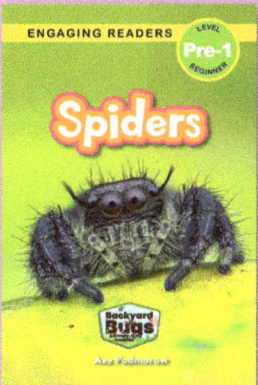

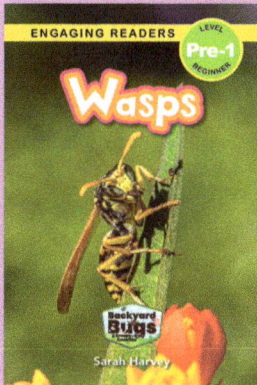

ENGAGING READERS — LEVEL Pre-1 BEGINNER

Ants — Backyard Bugs — Ava Podmorow

ENGAGING READERS — LEVEL Pre-1 BEGINNER

Beetles — Backyard Bugs — Victoria Hazlehurst

ENGAGING READERS — LEVEL Pre-1 BEGINNER

Caterpillars — Backyard Bugs — Ava Podmorow

ENGAGING READERS — LEVEL Pre-1 BEGINNER

Grasshoppers — Backyard Bugs — Ava Podmorow

ENGAGING READERS — LEVEL Pre-1 BEGINNER

Moths — Backyard Bugs — Ava Podmorow

ENGAGING READERS — LEVEL Pre-1 BEGINNER

Snails — Backyard Bugs — Ava Podmorow

ENGAGING READERS — LEVEL Pre-1 BEGINNER

Spiders — Backyard Bugs — Ava Podmorow

ENGAGING READERS — LEVEL Pre-1 BEGINNER

Wasps — Backyard Bugs — Sarah Harvey

ENGAGING READERS — LEVEL Pre-1 BEGINNER

Worms — Backyard Bugs — Victoria Hazlehurst

Visit www.engagebooks.com to explore more Engaging Readers.

Answers:
1. No 2. Yes 3. No 4. Yes 5. No 6. Yes